DOES GOD
Control
EVERYTHING?

The Crucial Questions Series
By R. C. Sproul

CRUCIAL
QUESTIONS
No. | 14

DOES GOD
Control
EVERYTHING?

R.C. SPROUL

R *Reformation Trust* A DIVISION OF LIGONIER MINISTRIES, ORLANDO, FL

Does God Control Everything?

© 2012 by R. C. Sproul

Published by Reformation Trust Publishing
a division of Ligonier Ministries
421 Ligonier Court, Sanford, FL 32771
Ligonier.org   ReformationTrust.com

Printed in North Mankato, MN
Corporate Graphics
August 2013
First edition, third printing

Cover design: Gearbox Studios
Interior design and typeset: Katherine Lloyd, The DESK

Library of Congress Cataloging-in-Publication Data

Sproul, R. C. (Robert Charles), 1939-
  Does God control everything? / R.C. Sproul.
    p. cm. -- (The crucial questions series ; no. 14)
  Includes bibliographical references.
  ISBN 978-1-56769-297-6
  1. Providence and government of God--Christianity. I. Title.
  BT135.S744 2012
  231'.5--dc23

                                            2012028858

Contents

Chapter One

WHAT IS
PROVIDENCE?

One day, while I was watching a news program, an advertisement appeared for a series of books about problems of life in the past. One of the images in the commercial depicted a Confederate soldier from the Civil War lying on a stretcher and receiving care from a nurse and a battle-line physician. The narrator then informed me that reading this book would help me understand what it was like to be sick in the mid-nineteenth century. That caught my attention, because many people of the twenty-first century are so strongly bound to this time that they rarely think about how people lived their daily lives in previous ages and generations.

This is one area where I find myself out of step with my contemporaries. I think about the lives of previous generations quite frequently, because I have a habit of reading books that were written by people who lived, in many cases, long before the twenty-first century. I particularly like to read the authors of the sixteenth, seventeenth, and eighteenth centuries.

In the writings of these authors I consistently notice an acute sense of the presence of God. These men had a sense of an overarching providence. We see an indication of that sense that all of life is under the direction and the governance of almighty God in the fact that one of the first cities in what is now the United States of America was Providence, Rhode Island (founded in 1636). Likewise, the personal correspondence from men of earlier centuries, such as Benjamin Franklin and John Adams, is laced with the word *providence*. People talked about a "benevolent Providence" or an "angry Providence," but often there was a sense that God was directly involved in the daily lives of people.

The situation is vastly different in our own day. My late friend James Montgomery Boice used to tell a humorous story that aptly illustrated the current mindset with regard to God and His involvement in the world. There was a mountain climber who slipped on a ledge and was about to plummet thousands of feet to his death, but as he started to fall, he grabbed a branch of a tiny, scraggly tree that was growing out of a crack in the face of the cliff. As he clung to the branch, the roots of the scraggly tree began to pull loose, and the climber was facing certain death. At that moment, he cried out to the heavens, "Is there anyone up there who can help me?" In reply, he heard a rich, baritone voice from the sky, saying: "Yes. I am here and I will help you. Let go of the branch and trust Me." The man looked up to heaven and then looked back down into the abyss. Finally, he raised his voice again and said, "Is there anyone else up there who can help me?"

I like that story because I think it typifies the cultural mentality of the present day. First, the climber asks, "Is there anyone up there?" Most eighteenth-century people assumed there *was* Someone up there. There was little doubt in their minds that an almighty Creator governed the affairs of the universe. But we live in a period of unprecedented skepticism about the very existence of God. Yes, polls regularly tell us that between ninety-five and ninety-eight percent of people in the United States believe in some kind of god or a higher power. I suppose that can be explained partly from the impact of tradition; ideas that have been precious to people for generations are hard to give up, and in our culture a certain social stigma is still attached to unbridled atheism. Also, I think we cannot escape the logic of assuming that there has to be some kind of foundational, ultimate cause for this world as we experience it. But usually, when we pin people down and begin to talk to them about their idea of a "higher power" or a "supreme being," it turns out to be a concept that is more of an "it" than a "He"—a kind of energy or an undefined force. That's why the climber asked, "Is there *anyone* up there?" In that moment of crisis, he recognized his need for a personal being who was in charge of the universe.

There is another aspect of that anecdote that I think is significant. When he was about to fall to his death, the climber did not simply ask, "Is there anyone up there?" He specified, "Is there anyone up there *who can help me*?" That is the question of modern man. He wants to know whether there is anyone outside the sphere of daily life who is able to be of assistance to him. But I think the climber was asking an even more fundamental question. He wanted to know not only whether there was someone who *could* help, but whether there was someone who was *willing* to help. This is the question that is foremost in the minds of modern men and women. In other words, they want to know not only whether there is providence, but whether it is cold and unfeeling or kind and compassionate.

So, the question of providence that I want to consider in this booklet is not merely whether there is anyone there, but whether that someone is able and willing to do anything in this world in which we live.

A CLOSED, MECHANISTIC UNIVERSE

Among the ideas that have shaped Western culture, one of the most significant is the idea of a closed, mechanistic universe. This view of the world has persisted for a couple of hundred years and has had tremendous influence in shaping how people understand the way life is lived out. I would argue that in the secular world, the dominant idea is that we live in a universe that is closed to any kind of intrusion from outside, a universe that runs purely by

mechanical forces and causes. In a word, the issue for modern man is *causality*.

There seems to be a growing outcry about the negative
influence of religion in American culture. Religion is held
to be the force that keeps people trapped in the dark ages
of superstition, their minds closed to any understanding of
the realities of the world that science has unveiled. More
and more, religion seems to be regarded as the polar oppo-
site of science and reason. It is as if science is something for
the mind, for research, and for intelligence, while religion
is something for the emotions and for feelings.

Yet, there is still a tolerance for religion. The idea is
often expressed in the news media that everyone has a right
to believe what he or she chooses to believe; the main thing
is to believe *something*. It does not matter whether you are
Jewish, Muslim, Buddhist, or Christian.

When I hear comments like that, I want to exclaim,
"Does truth matter at all?" The main thing, in my hum-
ble opinion, is to believe the truth. I am not satisfied to
believe just anything simply for the sake of believing. If
what I believe is not true—if it is superstitious or falla-
cious—I want to be liberated from it. But the mentality
of our day seems to be that in matters of religion, truth

is insignificant. We learn truth from science. We get good feelings from religion.

Sometimes the highly simplistic idea is set forth that religious superstition reigned supreme in the past, so God was seen as the cause of everything. If someone became sick, the illness was attributed to God. Now, of course, we are told that illnesses are due to microorganisms that invade our bodies, and those tiny organisms operate according to their nature, doing what they have evolved to do. Likewise, whereas in former days people believed an earthquake or a thunderstorm was caused by the hand of God, today we are assured that there are natural reasons for these events. They happen because of forces that are part of the natural order of things.

In the eighteenth century, a book was written that has become the classic of Western economic theory—*The Wealth of Nations*, by Adam Smith. In that book, Smith tried to apply the scientific method to the field of economics in an effort to discover what causes certain economic responses and counter-responses in the marketplace. Smith wanted to cut through speculation and identify basic causes that produced predictable effects. But even while he was applying this scientific inquiry to the complicated network of economic actions and reactions, he spoke of the "invisible hand." In other words, Smith was saying: "Yes, there are causes and effects going on in this world, but we have to recognize that above all there has to be an ultimate causal power or there would be no lower causal powers. Thus, the whole universe is orchestrated by the invisible hand of God." In our day, however, we have focused so intently on the immediate activity of cause and effect that for the most part we have ignored or denied the overarching causal power behind all of life. Modern man basically has no concept of providence.

THE GOD WHO SEES

The doctrine of providence is one of the most fascinating, important, and difficult doctrines in the Christian faith. It deals with difficult questions, such as: "How does God's causal power and authority interact with ours?" "How does God's sovereign rule relate to our free choices?" "How is God's government related to the evil and suffering in this world?" and "Does prayer have any influence over God's providential decisions?" In other words, how are we to live our lives in light of God's invisible hand?

Let us begin with a simple definition. The word *providence* has a prefix, *pro-*, which means "before" or "in front of." The root comes from the Latin verb *videre*, which means "to see"; it is from this word that we get our English word *video*. So, the word *providence* literally means "to see beforehand." The providence of God refers to His seeing something beforehand with respect to time.

Providence is not the same thing as God's foreknowledge or prescience. Foreknowledge is His ability to look down the corridors of time and know the outcome of an activity before it even begins. Nevertheless, it is appropriate to use the word *providence* with reference to God's active governance of the universe, because He is indeed a God who sees. He sees everything that takes place in the universe. It is in full view of His eyes.

This can be one of the most terrifying thoughts a human being can have—that there is someone who is, as Jean-Paul Sartre lamented, an ultimate cosmic voyeur who looks through the celestial keyhole and observes every action of every human being. If there is anything about the character of God that repels people from Him more than His holiness, it is His omniscience. Every one of us has a keen desire for a sense of privacy that no one can invade so as to pry into the secret things of our lives.

At the time of the first transgression, when sin entered the world, Adam and Eve immediately experienced a sense of nakedness and shame (Gen. 3:7). They reacted by attempting to hide from God (v. 8). They experienced the gaze of the God of providence. Like the mountain climber in my earlier anecdote, we want God to look at us when we need help. Most of the time, however, we want Him to overlook us, because we want privacy.

On one memorable occasion during the ministry of our Lord, the scribes and Pharisees dragged a woman they had caught in adultery into Jesus' presence. They reminded Him that the law of God required that she be stoned, but they wanted to know what He would do. But as they spoke, He bent down and wrote something on the ground. This is the only recorded instance of Jesus writing, and we do not know what He wrote. But we are told that He stood up and said, "Let him who is without sin among you be the first to throw a stone at her" (John 8:7). Then He began to write on the ground again. At that, the scribes and Pharisees began to go away, one by one.

I am speculating here, but I wonder whether Jesus wrote out some of the secret sins those men were zealous to keep locked away. Perhaps He wrote "adultery," and one of the men who was unfaithful to his wife read it and crept away. Perhaps he wrote "tax evasion," and one of the Pharisees who had failed to render unto Caesar decided to head for home. Jesus, in His divine nature, had the ability to see in a penetrating way behind the masks people wore, into the hiding places where they were most vulnerable. That is part of the concept of divine providence. It means that God knows everything about us.

As I noted above, we often find this divine sight disquieting, but the concept of God's vision, of God seeing us, should be comforting to us. Jesus said: "Are not two sparrows sold for a penny? And not one of them will fall to the ground apart from your Father" (Matt. 10:29). That teaching inspired the popular song "His Eye Is on the Sparrow." Do you remember the lyrics? "His eye is on the sparrow, and I know He watches me."[1] I believe the writer of that song understood what Jesus was saying—that God knows every time any tiny bird falls to the ground. God does not overlook even the slightest detail in the universe. Rather, He

---

1 From the song "His Eye Is on the Sparrow" by Civilla D. Martin and Charles H. Gabriel, 1905.

governs the universe in total awareness of everything that is happening within it.

Yes, this kind of intimate knowledge can be frightening. But because we know that God is benevolent and caring, His comprehensive knowledge is a comfort. He knows what we need before we ask Him. And when our needs arise, He is both able and willing to help us. To me, there is nothing more comforting than knowing that there is a God of providence who is aware not only of every one of my transgressions but of every one of my tears, every one of my aches, and every one of my fears.

Chapter Two

GOD MAKES IT ALL HAPPEN

One of the dominant concepts in Western culture for the past two hundred years, as we saw in the previous chapter, is that we live in a closed, mechanistic universe. The theory is that everything operates according to fixed natural laws, and that there is no possibility for intrusion from outside. So, the universe is like a machine that functions by its own inner machinations.

However, even those who introduced this concept as

early as the seventeenth century still posited the idea that God built the machine in the first place. Being intelligent thinkers and scientists, they could not get away from the need for a Creator. They recognized that there would be no world for them to observe if there were no ultimate cause for all things. Even though the idea of an involved, providential Governor of the daily affairs of life was questioned and challenged, it still was tacitly assumed that there had to be a Creator above and beyond the created order.

In the classical concept, God's providence was very closely bound up with His role as the Creator of the universe. No one believed that God simply created the universe and then turned His back on it and lost touch with it, or that He sat back on His throne in heaven and merely watched the universe work by its own inner mechanism, refusing to involve Himself in its affairs. Rather, the classical Christian notion was that God is both the primary cause of the universe and also the primary cause of everything that takes place in the universe.

One of the foundational principles of Christian theology is that nothing in this world has intrinsic causal power. Nothing has any power save the power that is vested in it—lent to it, if you will—or worked through it, which ultimately is the power of God. That is why theologians and philosophers historically have made a crucial distinction between primary causality and secondary causality.

God is the source of primary causality; in other words, He is the first cause. He is the Author of all that is, and He continues to be the primary cause of human events and of natural occurrences. However, His primary causality does not exclude secondary causes. Yes, when the rain falls, the grass gets wet, not because God makes the grass wet directly and immediately, but because the rain applies moisture to the grass. But the rain could not fall apart from the causal power of God that stands over and above every secondary causal activity. Modern man, however, is quick to say, "The grass is wet because the rain fell," and he looks no further for a higher, ultimate cause. Twenty-first-century people seem to think we can get along just fine with secondary causes and give no thought to the primary cause.

The basic concept here is that what God creates, He sustains. So, one of the important subdivisions in the doctrine of providence is the concept of divine sustenance. Simply put, this is the classical Christian idea that God is not the great Watchmaker who builds the watch, winds it up, and then steps out of the picture. Instead, what He makes, He preserves and sustains.

We actually see this at the very beginning of the Bible. Genesis 1:1 says, "In the beginning, God created the heavens and the earth." The Hebrew word translated as "created" is a form of the verb *bārā*, which means "to create, make." This word carries with it the idea of sustaining. I like to illustrate this idea by referencing the difference in music between a staccato note and a sustained note. A staccato note is short and crisp: "La la la la la." A sustained note is held: "Laaaa." Likewise, the word *bārā* tells us that God did not simply bring the world into existence in a moment. It indicates that He is continuing to make it, as it were. He is holding it, keeping it, and sustaining it.

THE AUTHOR OF BEING

One of the most profoundly important theological concepts is that God is the Author of being. We could not exist apart from a supreme being, because we do not have the power of being in and of ourselves. If any atheist would think seriously and logically about the concept of being for five minutes, it would be the end of his atheism. It is an inescapable fact that no one in this world has the power of being within himself, and yet we are here. So, somewhere there must be One who *does* have the power of being within Himself. If there is not such a One, it would be absolutely scientifically impossible for anything to be. If there is no supreme being, there could be no being of any kind. If there is something, there must be something that has the power of being; otherwise, nothing would be. It's that simple.

When the Apostle Paul spoke to the philosophers at the Areopagus in Athens, he mentioned that he had seen many altars in the city, including one to "the unknown god" (Acts 17:23a). He then used that as an opening to speak biblical truth to them: "What therefore you worship as unknown, this I proclaim to you. The God who made the world and everything in it . . . gives to all mankind life and breath and everything . . . for 'In him we live and move and have our being'" (vv. 23b–28a). Paul said that everything God creates is completely dependent on God's power, not only for its origin but for the continuity of its existence.

Sometimes I am impatient with some of the poetic

liberties that hymn writers take. One famous hymn includes this line: "Amazing love! How can it be that thou, my God, shouldst die for me?"[2] Yes, God died on the cross in a manner of speaking. The God-man, the One who was God incarnate, died for His people. But the divine nature did not perish at Calvary. What would happen to the universe if God died? If God ceased to exist, the universe would perish with Him, because God not only has created everything, He sustains everything. We are dependent on Him, not only for our origin, but also for our continuing existence. Since we do not have the power of being in and of ourselves, we could not last for a second without His sustaining power. That is part of God's providence.

This idea that God sustains the world—the world that He made and observes in intimate detail—brings us to the heart of the concept of providence, which is the teaching that God governs His creation. This teaching has many aspects, but I want to focus on three in the remainder of this chapter—the truths that God's government of all things is permanent, sovereign, and absolute.

---

2   From the hymn "And Can It Be That I Should Gain" by Charles Wesley, 1738.

A PERMANENT GOVERNMENT

Every few years, we have a change of government in the United States as a new presidential administration takes over. The Constitution limits the number of years a president may serve as the chief executive of the United States. So, by human standards, governments come and go. Any time a president comes into office, the news media mentions the "honeymoon period," that time when the new leader is looked upon with favor, warmly received, and so on. But as more and more people become annoyed or disappointed with his policies, his popularity falls. Soon, we hear some pundits opining that we need to throw the "bum" out of office. In other countries, such dissatisfaction has occasionally resulted in armed revolution, resulting in the violent overthrow of presidents or prime ministers. In any case, no earthly ruler retains power forever.

God, however, is seated as the supreme Governor of heaven and earth. He, too, must put up with people who are disenchanted with His rule, who object to His policies, and who resist His authority. But even though God's very existence can be denied, His authority can be resisted, and His laws disobeyed, His providential government can never be overthrown.

Psalm 2 gives us a vivid picture of God's secure reign. The psalmist writes: "Why do the nations rage and the peoples plot in vain? The kings of the earth set themselves, and the rulers take counsel together, against the Lord and against his anointed, saying, 'Let us burst their bonds apart and cast away their cords from us'" (vv. 1–3). The image here is that of a summit meeting of the powerful rulers of this world. They come together to enter into a coalition, a kind of military axis, to plan the overthrow of divine authority. It is as if they are planning to fire their nuclear missiles at the throne of God so as to blast Him out of heaven. Their goal is to be free of divine authority, to throw off the "bonds" and "cords" with which God binds them. But the conspiracy is not just against "the Lord," it is also against "his anointed." The Hebrew word here is *māšîah*, from which we get our English word *Messiah*. God the Father has exalted His Son as head over all things, with the right to rule the rulers of this world. Those who are invested with earthly authority are taking counsel together to plan how to rid the universe of the authority of God and His Son.

What is God's reaction to this earthly conspiracy? The psalmist says, "He who sits in the heavens laughs; the Lord holds them in derision" (v. 4). The kings of the earth set themselves in opposition to God. They agree with solemn pacts and treaties, and they encourage one another not to waver from their resolve to overthrow the King of the universe. But when God looks down at all these assembled powers, He does not tremble in fear. He laughs, but not the laughter of amusement. The psalmist describes the laughter of God as the laughter of derision. It is the laughter that a powerful king expresses when he holds his enemies in contempt.

But God does not merely laugh: "Then he will speak to them in his wrath, and terrify them in his fury, saying, 'As for me, I have set my King on Zion, my holy hill'" (vv. 5–6). God will rebuke the rebellious nations and affirm the King He has seated in Zion.

I am frequently amazed at the difference between the accent I find in the pages of sacred Scripture and that which I read in the pages of religious magazines and hear preached in the pulpits of our churches. We have an image of God as full of benevolence. We see Him as a celestial bellhop we can call when we need room service or as a cosmic Santa

Claus who is ready to shower us with gifts. He is pleased to do whatever we ask Him to do. Meanwhile, He gently pleads with us to change our ways and to come to His Son, Jesus. We do not usually hear about a God who commands obedience, who asserts His authority over the universe and insists we bow down to His anointed Messiah. Yet, in Scripture, we never see God inviting people to come to Jesus. He commands us to repent and convicts us of treason at a cosmic level if we choose not to do so. A refusal to submit to the authority of Christ probably will not land anyone in trouble with the church or the government, but it will certainly create a problem with God.

In the Upper Room Discourse (John 13–17), Jesus told His disciples that He was going away, but He promised to send them another Helper (14:16), the Holy Spirit. He said, "When he comes, he will convict the world concerning sin and righteousness and judgment" (16:8). When Jesus spoke about the Spirit coming to convict the world of sin, He became very specific about the sin He had in mind. It was the sin of unbelief. He said the Spirit would bring conviction "concerning sin, because they do not believe in me" (v. 9). From God's perspective, refusal to submit to the lordship of Christ is not simply due to a lack of conviction or a lack of information. God regards it as unbelief, as a failure to accept the Son of God for who He is.

Paul echoed this idea at the Areopagus when he said, "The times of ignorance God overlooked, but now he commands all people everywhere to repent" (Acts 17:30). God had been patient, Paul said, but He now commanded everyone to repent and believe in Christ. We rarely hear this idea in print or from the pulpit, the idea that it is our duty to submit to Christ. But while we may not hear it, it is not an option with God.

Simply put, God reigns supreme over His universe, and His reign will never end.

A SOVEREIGN GOVERNMENT

In the United States, we live in a democracy, so it is difficult for us to understand the idea of sovereignty. Our social contract declares that no one can govern here except by the consent of the governed. But God does not need our consent in order to govern us. He made us, so He has an intrinsic right to rule over us.

In the Middle Ages, the monarchs of Europe sought to ground their authority in the so-called "divine right of kings." They declared that they had a God-given right to rule over their countrymen. In truth, only God has such a right.

In England, the power of the monarch, once very great, is now limited. England is a constitutional monarchy. The queen enjoys all the pomp and circumstance of royalty, but Parliament and the prime minister run the nation, not Buckingham Palace. The queen reigns but she does not rule.

By contrast, the biblical King both reigns and rules. And He carries out His rule not by referendum but by His personal sovereignty.

AN ABSOLUTE GOVERNMENT

God's government is an absolute monarchy. No external restraints are imposed on Him. He does not have to respect a balance of powers with a Congress and a Supreme Court. God is the President, the Senate, the House, and the Supreme Court all wrapped into one, because He is invested with the authority of an absolute monarch.

The history of the Old Testament is the history of the reign of Yahweh over His people. The central motif of the New Testament is the realization on earth of the kingdom of God in the Messiah, whom God exalts to the right hand of authority and crowns as the King of kings and Lord of lords. He is the ultimate Ruler, the One to whom we owe ultimate allegiance and ultimate obedience.

One of the great ironies of history is that when Jesus, who was the cosmic King, was born in Bethlehem, the world was ruled by a man named Caesar Augustus. Properly speaking, however, the word *august* is appropriate for God alone. It means "of supreme dignity or grandeur; majestic; venerable; eminent." God is the superlative fulfillment of all these terms, for the Lord God omnipotent reigns.

Chapter Three

GOD OR
CHANCE?

Following the Israelites' exodus from Egypt, God commanded His people to build a tabernacle, a large tent that would function as the center of their worship. The innermost section of the tabernacle, which was curtained off, was the Holy of Holies, into which only the high priest could go, and only on one day each year, the Day of Atonement. It was there, in the Holy of Holies, that the ark of the covenant was kept. The ark was not a boat, as in the story of Noah's ark, but a large, gold-covered chest. Inside the chest were kept the tablets of the Ten Commandments, Aaron's rod that had budded, and a pot of the manna with which God miraculously fed the people in the wilderness (Heb. 9:4). The lid of the ark, which was adorned with two golden cherubim, was regarded as the throne of God. Simply put, the ark was the most sacred vessel in all of Jewish religious history.

It also had military significance for the Jews. When Moses and Joshua led the Israelites in their journey to the Promised Land and in their conquest of Canaan, when they went into battle against their enemies, the priests carried the ark of the covenant. When the throne of God accompanied the armies of Israel, they were victorious. God was with them in battle and fought for them.

Sadly, the people eventually began to associate victory in battle with the ark itself, not with God. We see this in 1 Samuel 4, which recounts an occasion when the Israelites went into battle with the Philistines (but not accompanied by the ark) and suffered defeat, with the loss of four thousand men. We then read: "When the people came to the camp, the elders of Israel said, 'Why has the LORD defeated us today before the Philistines? Let us bring the ark of the covenant of the LORD here from Shiloh, that it may come among us and save us from the power of our enemies" (v. 3). The people attributed their defeat to God, but they looked to the ark to save them.

So, the ark was brought to the Israelite camp. When the soldiers saw the arrival of the throne of God, they gave a tumultuous, thunderous cheer. Across the valley, the Philistines heard this cheer, and when they discovered the reason for it, they knew they were in deep trouble, for they remembered how God had struck the Egyptians during the exodus (vv. 5–8).

At this time, Israel was led by Eli, a priest and judge. He was a godly man who had served the people for decades, but he had one serious defect. He had two sons, Hophni and Phinehas, who also were priests, but they did not share Eli's godliness, and they committed all kinds of desecration of their sacred vocation. However, Eli never disciplined them. So, God had spoken to Eli through a prophet, warning him that judgment was going to fall on his house, for Hophni and Phinehas would die on the same day (2:30–34).

This prophecy came to fulfillment when the Israelites, jubilant to have the ark of God with them, went back into battle with the Philistines, and Hophni and Phinehas accompanied the ark. The unthinkable happened—the Israelites did *not* prevail, even though the ark was present. This time, thirty thousand Israelite men fell (4:10). Hophni and Phinehas also died, but worst of all, the pagan Philistines captured the ark of the covenant (v. 11).

After the battle, a messenger ran back to Shiloh with the bad news. Eli was ninety-eight years old, and he was blind and overweight (vv. 15, 18). He was seated by the gate where he issued judgments, for he was waiting anxiously for news of the battle. When the messenger came and told him that Israel was defeated, his sons were dead, and the ark was captured, Eli fell over backward, broke his neck, and died (v. 18).

Eli's daughter-in-law, the wife of Phinehas, was pregnant and about to give birth. When she heard the news of the defeat and the death of her husband, she went into labor. She gave birth to a son, but she died as a result of her labor. Before she died, however, she named the boy Ichabod, a name that means "the glory has departed" (vv. 19–22). That baby boy was born on the day when Israel's greatest glory, the throne of God, was taken into captivity by the pagan Philistines.

AFFLICTIONS FOR THE PHILISTINES

The Philistines, we are told, took the ark to Ashdod, one of their five city-states. They took it into their most holy temple, which was devoted to Dagon, their principal deity. In the temple, they placed the ark at the feet of an image of Dagon, the place of humiliation and subordination (5:1–2). The next morning, however, they found the statue of Dagon fallen on its face; it was as if Dagon was prostrate before the throne of Yahweh. The priests propped their deity back up, but the next morning, the statue not only had fallen over on its face, its head and hands were broken off (vv. 3–4).

To make matters worse, a plague of tumors broke out in Ashdod (v. 6), and, apparently, a plague of mice (6:5). The men of Ashdod suspected that these afflictions were coming from the hand of God, so they convened a council to debate what to do. The decision was made to send the ark to another of the Philistine city-states, Gath (5:7–8). However, the same afflictions began in Gath, so the people of Gath decided to send the ark to Ekron. But news of the afflictions had preceded the ark, and the people of Ekron refused to receive it. After seven months of trials, the Philistines finally realized that the ark had to be sent back to Israel (5:9–6:1).

Returning such a sacred object to Israel was no simple task. The Philistines assembled their priests and diviners to advise them as to how to do it. The priests and diviners recommended they send it back with a "guilt offering"—five golden tumors and five golden mice (6:2–6).

Now the story gets interesting. The priests and diviners told the Philistine leaders to prepare a new cart and to put the ark and the golden tumors and mice on it. Then they were to find two milk cows that had never been yoked and hitch them to the cart. Finally, they were to take the cows' calves away from them. Once all this was done, they were to release the cart but watch where the cows took it. They said, "If it goes up on the way to its own land, to Beth-shemesh, then it is [Israel's God] who has done us this great harm, but if not, then we shall know that it is not his hand that struck us; it happened to us by coincidence" (v. 9). In essence, then, this was an elaborate experiment to see whether God had been behind the afflictions or whether they had happened by "chance."

It is vital that we understand how the Philistines "stacked

the deck," as it were, to determine conclusively whether it was the God of Israel that had caused their afflictions.

They found cows that had just calved. What is the natural inclination for a mother cow that has just given birth? If you take that mother cow away from her calf and then let her go free, she is going to make a beeline to her calf. Likewise, they chose cows that had never been yoked or trained to pull a cart in a yoke. In such a case, a cow is likely to struggle against the yoke and is unlikely to work well with the other cow in the yoke. With these issues built into the experiment, it was very unlikely the cart would go anywhere, least of all toward the land of Israel. If the cows were able to pull the cart at all, they would want to return to their calves. So, if the cart went toward Israel, that would be a sign that God was guiding the cows—and therefore that He had orchestrated the afflictions that had come on the Philistines since their capture of the ark.

AN EXPERIMENT OF ATHEISTS

This experiment sounds primitive. It took place in the pre-scientific era. These people were not sophisticated. They did not have PhDs in physics. Their naiveté as they tried to discern the cause of their affliction is amusing. But there is something about this story that I find exceedingly contemporary—these people clearly were atheists. You may be surprised by that statement, because the Bible tells us the Philistines had a temple, a priesthood, and a religion, as part of which they engaged in religious activities. Why, then, do I make the assertion that they were atheists?

Years ago, when I was teaching at a seminary, I was responsible to teach a course on the theology of the Westminster Confession of Faith, which is a seventeenth-century theological document that is the confessional foundation for historic Presbyterianism. The first two chapters of the confession deal with the Scriptures and with the triune God, while the third chapter is titled "Of God's Eternal Decree." Presbyterians know exactly what that means—predestination. Seminary students enjoy chewing over difficult doctrinal questions, and they especially enjoy debating predestination, so there was excitement about my pending lecture on this doctrine. Most of my students invited friends who did not believe in predestination, so when the class met to consider this difficult doctrine, about twice the usual number of people were assembled.

I started the class by reading the opening lines of chapter

three of the Westminster Confession: "God, from all eternity, did, by the most wise and holy counsel of His own will, freely and unchangeably ordain whatsoever comes to pass." Then I paused and said: "The confession says that from all eternity God freely and unchangeably has ordained everything that comes to pass. How many of you believe that?" This was a Presbyterian seminary, so many hands went up; the good Presbyterian students in the class were proud to confess their conviction about the sovereignty of God.

Of course, not everyone raised his hand, so I asked: "How many of you don't believe this? Nobody's taking down names. You're not going to get in any trouble. We're not going to have a heresy trial here and get out the matches and burn you at the stake. Just be honest." Finally, a number of fellows raised their hands. When they did, I said: "Let me ask another question: How many of you would candidly describe yourselves as atheists? Again, be honest." No one raised his hand, so I said: "I don't understand why those of you who said you do not agree with the confession did not raise your hands when I asked you if you were atheists."

As you can imagine, there was a hue and cry from the students who did not agree with the confession. They were ready to lynch me. They said: "What are you talking about? Just because we don't believe that God ordains everything that comes to pass, you're calling us atheists?" I said: "That's exactly what I'm calling you. If you don't believe that God ordains everything that comes to pass, you don't believe in God." I then went on to explain to them that the passage I had read from the confession did not say anything uniquely Presbyterian. It was not even uniquely Christian. That statement did not divide Presbyterians from Methodists, Lutherans, or Anglicans, and it did not distinguish between Presbyterians, Muslims, or Jews. It simply offered a distinction between theism and atheism.

What I wanted these young people to see was this: if God is not sovereign, God is not God. If there is even one maverick molecule in the universe—one molecule running loose outside the scope of God's sovereign ordination—we cannot have the slightest confidence that any promise God has ever made about the future will come to pass.

This, then, is why I say the Philistines were atheists. They allowed for the possibility of an event in this world caused by chance—the possibility that, against all the evidence, the afflictions they had endured had happened by coincidence. They were allowing for a maverick molecule, so they were allowing for the possibility of a God who is not sovereign, and a God who is not sovereign is not God.

The great message of atheism is that "chance" has causal power. Again and again the view is expressed that we do not need to attribute the creation of the universe to God, for we know that it came to be through space plus time plus chance. This is nonsense; there is nothing that chance can do. Chance is a perfectly good word to describe mathematic possibilities, but it is only a word. It is not an entity. Chance is nothing. It has no power because it has no being; therefore, it can exercise no influence over anything. Yet, we have sophisticated scientists today who make sober statements declaring that the whole universe was created by chance. This is to say that nothing caused something, and there is no statement more anti-scientific than that. Everything has a cause, and the ultimate cause, as we have seen, is God.

When the Philistines let the cows go, they "went straight in the direction of Beth-shemesh along one highway, lowing as they went. They turned neither to the right nor to the left" (6:12). The cows pulled the cart smoothly, even though they had never been yoked. They walked away from their calves, even though they wished to go to them, as evidenced by their lowing. And they went straight toward Israel. Did all that happen by chance? No, the cows were guided by the invisible hand of the God of providence. Thus, the Philistines knew that that same hand had afflicted them.

Chapter Four

IS GOD RESPONSIBLE FOR HUMAN WICKEDNESS?

On February 12, 1938, two men had a private meeting in a mountain retreat. In the course of their conversation, one of the men said to the other, "I have a historic mission, and this mission I will fulfill, because Providence has destined me to do so."[3] This man had an understanding

---

3 Adolf Hitler, cited in William L. Shirer, *The Rise and Fall of the Third Reich: A History of Nazi Germany*, 3rd edition (New York: Simon & Schuster, 1990), 326.

that the purpose of his life was under the shaping influence of divine providence. He went on to say to the other gentleman in the course of their conversation that anyone "who is not with me will be crushed."[4]

The man who made this claim to a providential destiny was Adolf Hitler. Similarly, when Joseph Stalin was elevated to the role of premier of the Soviet Union, the bishops of the Russian Orthodox Church rejoiced in this stroke of providence, as they were convinced that God had raised Stalin up to be a divine instrument for the leadership of the people of Russia. Yet today, when people discuss the diabolical evils that have been perpetrated on the human race, two of the names we hear most frequently associated with human wickedness are those of Hitler and Stalin.

Whenever we study the doctrine of providence and the question of divine government, we inevitably hear that the Scriptures teach us that God lifts nations up and brings nations down (Dan. 2:21; 4:17; Rom. 13:1). This raises a question: How is divine providence related to evil governments, evil individuals, and indeed the whole question of evil? In the previous chapter, I quoted from the third

4 Ibid.

chapter of the Westminster Confession of Faith, which says, "God, from all eternity, did, by the most wise and holy counsel of His own will, freely and unchangeably ordain whatsoever comes to pass." Does that mean, then, that God ordained Hitler and Stalin? Is evil ordained by the providence of God?

It has been said that the existence of evil and the difficulty of explaining it in light of the concept of a sovereign God who is supposed to be good is the "Achilles' heel" of Christianity. According to Greek mythology, when Achilles was born, his mother dipped him in the River Styx in an attempt to make him immortal. But when she dipped him, she held him by the heel, and that part of his body was not immersed, and therefore was not invincible. Eventually, he was killed when he received an arrow wound in his heel during the Trojan War. Those who argue that the problem of evil is the Achilles' heel of Christianity mean that it is Christianity's most vulnerable spot. If God ordains everything that comes to pass, it seems that He must ordain evil. And if God ordains evil, the argument goes, He Himself is evil.

The philosopher John Stuart Mill (1806–1873) used this argument in his objections to Christianity. He wrote, "Not even on the most distorted and contracted theory of good which ever was framed by religious or philosophical fanaticism, can the government of Nature be made to resemble the work of a being at once good and omnipotent.[5] He was saying that because of the undeniable reality of evil, he could not conceive of a God who was both all-powerful and all-righteous.

Of course, some try to resolve this difficulty by denying the reality of evil. Mary Baker Eddy, the founder of Christian Science, said evil is an illusion. I once had a debate with a Christian Science teacher about the question of evil. He insisted that evil is an illusion, that it does not really exist, while I insisted that evil is real. At one point in the discussion, I said: "Let me see if we can recapitulate where we stand. You say that evil is an illusion. I say that it's real. Do you think I'm real?" He said yes. I then asked, "Do you understand that I'm saying that evil is real and you're saying it's an illusion?" He said he understood that. I went on: "Do you think it's a good thing that I'm teaching people that evil is real?" He said he did not think so. Finally I asked, "Do you think it's evil for me to teach people that

---

5 John Stuart Mill, *Three Essays on Religion* (New York: Henry Holt & Co., 1874), 38.

evil is real?" He did not know what to say at that point. He had to conclude that I was an illusion as well.

THE CAUSE AND THE EFFECT

I noted in chapter one that the key issue for modern man is causality, and this question is nowhere more acute than when we talk about the problem of evil. When I was a freshman in college, only a few months after I became a Christian, I was playing Ping-Pong one day in my dorm, and right in the middle of a volley a thought (which was in no way original) came to me: "If God is all-righteous, He's capable only of good; so, how could He possibly have created a world that is marred with evil? If God is the source of all things and He's good, how could there be evil?" That problem troubled me deeply then and it has troubled me even more since, and it troubles many other people, too.

As I began to ponder these things and to study the question of causality, I studied, and later taught, seventeenth-century philosophy. The most prominent philosopher during that time was the French mathematician and scholar René Descartes. He was very concerned about reasoning from causality. He argued for the existence of the world by saying that the universe requires a sufficient cause, a cause that is able to give the result that we now observe. So, he argued from cause to effect to the existence of God, reasoning backward from the universe to God. One of the principles he used in that argument for the existence of God was this: "There can be nothing in the effect that is not first in the cause." To state it another way, "There cannot be more in the effect than inheres in the cause."

That principle, which has been espoused by thinkers for millennia, is a valid one, and it is critical to other arguments for the existence of God. For example, one argument that we use to prove the existence of God is the argument from human personality. We can prove that there has to be a first cause, that this first cause has to be self-existent and eternal, and so on. But after we do that, people will often say, "How do we know that this first cause is personal?" One of the ways I respond to this question is to ask: "Are we persons? Is there such a thing as personality, which involves volition, intelligence, affection—the things that are so integral to what we are as human beings?" If people agree that human beings are personal, that they have intelligence, intentionality, volition, and so on, I can reply: "Well, we cannot have an impersonal source for personality. There has to be personality in the cause if there is personality in the effect."

But that particular argument, as valid as it may be, can backfire on the Christian. Critics of Christianity have responded that if there cannot be more in the effect than is inherent in the cause, then God must be evil, because if we have an effect here that is evil, and if there cannot be more in the effect than is inherent in the cause, evil must exist in the cause.

How do we respond to this argument? The simple answer is that there is something in the creature that does not reside in the Creator—sin. That does not mean that the creature has something greater than the Creator; rather, the creature has something far less than the Creator.

A DEFINITION OF EVIL

To explain what I mean, I want to turn to the historic definition of evil. What is evil? To be clear, I am not talking about natural evil or metaphysical evil; rather, I'm talking about moral evil. Human beings have at least this much in common with God—we are moral creatures. We are capable of actions that may be deemed right or wrong. Of course, we live in a time when many people deny that proposition. They say that nothing is objectively good or evil. Instead, there are only preferences, which means that everything is relative. Good and evil are simply societal conventions that we have received through various traditions.

Years ago, I endured a calamity of the highest magnitude—my golf clubs were stolen. That theft was particularly distressing to me because the clubs were in a new golf bag my wife had given to me, so it had sentimental value. Also, I had two specially built clubs that a friend who is on the PGA Tour had given to me. Now, I am a theologian. I am supposed to know something about sin. I think I have seen every kind of human frailty there is under the sun, and I understand the temptations that go with our humanness. But candidly, I have never quite been able to understand the mentality of people who steal, who actually have the audacity to take for themselves someone else's private property. One man works long hours each week, earning wages by the sweat of his brow so he can purchase a certain commodity that he wants or needs. Another man, seeing something he wants or needs, simply takes it for himself with no investment of time or effort. I cannot understand that mindset. Even though we are masters of self-justification, experts at coming up with excuses for our sins, I cannot conceive of how a thief can look at himself in a mirror and see anything other than a person who is unspeakably selfish and self-centered. In short, I am astonished at how evil people can be. As you can see, I am not in the camp of those who believe theft is not objectively wrong.

We do not need a complex philosophical argument to prove the evil of stealing. It is self-evident. People know instinctively that stealing someone else's property is wrong. I might say that there is no such thing as evil and argue about it philosophically, but the argument ends when someone helps himself to my wallet. Then I say: "That's not right. That's not good. That's bad."

But what is evil? The Westminster Shorter Catechism defines sin this way: "Sin is any want of conformity unto, or transgression of, the law of God" (Q&A 14). Here, the confession defines sin or evil in both a negative and a positive way. There are sins of omission and sins of commission. But I want to zero in on the first part of the definition, "any want of conformity unto . . . the law of God." The word "want" here does not mean "desire" but "lack." So, sin is a lack of conformity to the standard God establishes for righteousness.

The ancient philosophers defined evil in terms of "negation" and "privation." That is, evil is the negation of the good and a privation (or lack) of goodness. Something that falls short of the plentitude of righteousness is evil. The philosophers were showing that the only way we can describe and define evil is in negative terms. This means that evil, by its very nature, is parasitic. It depends upon its host for its existence. This is what Augustine had in mind when he said that only something good can do that which is evil because the evil requires volition, intelligence, and a moral sense or awareness—all of which are good. So, something happens to a good being that indicates a loss, a lack, or a denial of goodness.

Augustine took the position that it is impossible to conceive of a being that is completely evil. Yes, Satan is radically evil, but he was created as an angel, which means he was part of the creation that God saw as very good. So, even Satan was created good, just as men were created good. Thus, at the point of creation, the eternal God, who is altogether good, acted as a moral agent to create other moral agents that were good. But the great difference between the Creator and the creature is that God is eternally, immutably good, whereas the creature was made mutably good. That is, he was made with the possibility of changing in his conformity to the law of God.

We see, then, that we cannot understand disobedience without first having a concept of obedience. Lawlessness is defined by lawfulness. Unrighteousness depends upon a prior definition of righteousness. The antichrist cannot exist apart from his antithetical relationship to Christ. We understand that evil is defined as a negation or a lack of conformity to the standards of the good.

THE ORDINATION OF EVIL

The supreme question is this: "Does God do evil?" The Bible is absolutely clear: God is absolutely incapable of performing evil. Yet, we have affirmed that God ordains everything that comes to pass, and some of the things that come to pass are evil. So, does God ordain evil? There is only one biblical answer to that question: yes. If God did not ordain evil, there would be no evil, because God is sovereign.

We trip and stumble over the word *ordain*. We think that affirming divine ordination of all things must mean that God either does evil or imposes it on righteous creatures, forcing innocent people to do sinful deeds. No. He ordained that His creatures should have the capacity for evil. He did not force them to exercise that capacity, but He knew that they would exercise it. At that point, He had a choice. He could destroy the creation so as not to allow evil to happen. The moment the Serpent came to Adam and Eve and began to suggest disobedience, God could have snuffed out the Serpent or snuffed out Adam and Eve. There would have been no sin. But God, for reasons known only to Himself, made the decision to let it happen. God did not sanction it, but He did not stop it. In choosing not to stop it, He ordained it.

I have to say that I have no idea why God allows evil to besmirch His universe. However, I know that when God ordains anything, His purpose is altogether good. Does this mean I think that in the final analysis evil really is good? No. I am saying it must be good that evil exists, because God sovereignly, providentially ordains only what is good. In terms of His eternal purpose, God has esteemed it good that evil should be allowed to happen in this world.

That does not mean that the sins that I commit, insofar as they contribute to God's providential plan and government of world history, are actually virtues. Judas' treachery was part of the divine providence in God's plan for redeeming the world. Judas could not have delivered Christ to Pilate apart from the providential decree of God. We know that this was the predetermined counsel of God, and yet God did not put evil into the heart of Judas. God did not coerce Judas to do his diabolical sin. Therefore, Judas cannot stand up on the last day and say, "If it hadn't been for me, there would have been no cross, no atonement, and no salvation—I'm the one who made it all possible." What Judas did was utterly evil, but when God ordains all things that come to pass, He ordains not only the ends but also the means to those ends, and He works through all things to bring about His righteous purpose.

One of the most comforting verses of Scripture is Romans 8:28: "And we know that for those who love God all things work together for good, for those who are called according to His purpose." Only a God of sovereign providence could make a promise like that. This statement does not mean that all things *are* good, but that all things work together *for* good. They can work together for good only because, over and above all evil, all acts of human wickedness, stands a sovereign God who has appointed a destiny both for the universe and for us as individuals, and that destiny is perfectly consistent with His righteousness.

Chapter Five

WHAT ABOUT
HUMAN FREEDOM?

In an earlier chapter, we briefly considered the provocative first line of the Westminster Confession's chapter "On God's Eternal Decree," which says: "God, from all eternity, did, by the most wise and holy counsel of His own will, freely and unchangeably ordain whatsoever comes to pass; yet so, as thereby neither is God the author of sin, nor is violence offered to the will of the creatures; nor is the liberty or contingency of second causes taken away, but rather established." The theologians who were involved in putting together that doctrinal statement were careful to say that even though we believe in a sovereign God who governs all things and ordains whatsoever comes to pass, His sovereign, providential government is not exercised in such a way as to destroy what we call human freedom or human volition. Rather, human choices and human actions are a part of the overall providential scheme of things, and God brings His will to pass by means of the free decisions of moral agents. The fact that our free decisions fit into this overarching plan in no way lessens the reality of that freedom.

Still, the question of how our free decisions correspond to God's sovereign providence is one of the most excruciatingly difficult questions with which we struggle in theology. Years ago, I engaged in a discussion with a professor from Carnegie Mellon University. At that time, he taught in the physics department, and he was somewhat hostile toward theology, seeing it as more or less a pseudoscience. He said, "At the very heart of your belief system are things that are simply indefinable." When I asked him to name some examples, he said: "God. What is more basic to theology than God? And yet, anything that you can say about God is ultimately imprecise." I replied: "Our first doctrine about God is what we call the 'incomprehensibility of God'—that no concept can exhaustively describe Him. But that doesn't mean that the statements we make about Him are totally inadequate. Surely you can be sympathetic with our struggle in the science of theology because you have to deal with the same problem in physics." He denied that physicists had any such problem and asked me to explain. I said: "What is energy? How basic is energy to modern physics?" He said, "I can answer that question—energy is the ability to do work." I said: "No, I'm not asking you what energy can do. I'm asking you what it is." He said, "OK, energy is MC^2." I said: "No, I don't want its mathematical equivalency. I want its ontological structure." He finally sighed and said, "I see what you mean."

It is a human tendency to think we can solve a metaphysical mystery by putting a name to it or giving it a definition. There is no one out there, at least no one of whom I am aware, who understands gravity. Likewise, I do not know any scientist who has yet answered the oldest, most perplexing philosophical and scientific question: "What is motion?" Putting a label on something or attaching a technical term to it does not explain everything about it.

THE DOCTRINE OF CONCURRENCE

I have gone into this lengthy point because we have a word for the relationship between divine sovereign providence and human freedom, but while I think it is a useful word, it is merely descriptive; it does not explain how human actions and divine providence square. The word is *concurrence*. Concurrence refers to the actions of two or more parties taking place at the same time. One string of actions occurs with another string, and they happen to dovetail or converge in history. So, the Christian doctrine of the relationship between God's sovereignty and human volitional actions is called the doctrine of concurrence. As you can see, the word *concurrence* simply designates this process, but it does not explain it.

I think one of the finest illustrations of concurrence is found in the Old Testament book of Job. This book is presented somewhat in the form of a drama, and the opening scene took place in heaven. Satan entered the scene after going to and fro across the earth, canvassing the performance of men who were supposed to be devoted to God. God asked Satan, "Have you considered my servant Job, that there is none like him on the earth, a blameless and upright man, who fears God and turns away from evil?" (1:8). Of course, Satan was cynical. He said to God: "Does Job fear God for no reason? Have you not put a hedge around him and his house and all that he has, on every side? You have blessed the work of his hands, and his possessions have increased in the land" (vv. 9b–10). Satan's questions implied that Job was faithful and loyal to his Creator only because of what he got from God. So, Satan challenged God: "But stretch out your hand and touch all that he has, and he will curse you to your face" (v. 11). Therefore, God gave Satan permission to attack all Job's possessions and, later, Job's health.

How did Satan carry out his attack on Job? We are told that, among other events, the Chaldeans took his camels (v. 17). So, in this theft, three agents were involved—the Chaldeans, Satan, and God. Let us consider each of these agents one by one.

Some scholars, focusing on Satan's malicious intent, conclude that the Chaldeans were upright men who respected Job, but demonic forces under the control of Satan drove them to steal Job's camels. They had no thought of stealing from Job until Satan put the idea into their minds. But Scripture never makes such a claim. The truth is that the Chaldeans were camel-rustlers from the beginning. They had a covetous, envious, jealous rage against Job, and the only thing that had kept the Chaldeans out of Job's corral for years was the protective hedge God had placed around Job. Given the chance, however, they were more than happy to take Job's camels.

Satan was not interested in seeing the Chaldeans pick up a few free camels. His goal in this drama was to force Job to curse God. He was acting with malice and malevolence to overthrow the authority and the majesty of God. He hoped that the theft of Job's camels by the Chaldeans would be a step toward that goal. So there was an agreement in purpose between the Chaldeans and Satan.

However, there was a total disagreement between the purposes of the Chaldeans and Satan and the purpose of God. Based on what we have learned so far about providence, we can safely conclude that God ordained that Job's camels be stolen. That was God's providential plan. But God's purpose was to vindicate Job from the unrighteous accusations of Satan, as well as to vindicate His own holiness.

Was it a legitimate purpose for God to vindicate Job? Was it a legitimate purpose for Him to vindicate His own holiness? I am not saying that the end justifies the means, but God's purposes and designs have to be considered in our evaluation of this drama. God did not sin against Job. Righteousness did not require that God keep Job from ever losing his camels. Remember, Job was a sinner. He had no eternal claim to those camels. Any camels that Job possessed were gifts of God's grace, and God had every right under heaven to remove or to repeal that grace for His own holy purposes. So, in this drama, God acted rightly, but Satan and the Chaldeans did evil. One event, three agents, three different purposes.

CONCURRENCE IN THE STORY OF JOSEPH

My favorite illustration of concurrence is the story of Joseph, which we find in the latter chapters of Genesis. Joseph was favored by his father, Jacob, who gave Joseph a colorful coat. Joseph's brothers hated him because of this favored treatment (37:3–4). One day, when Joseph fell into his brothers' hands far from their father's watching eyes, they went so far as to discuss killing him, but in the end they simply sold him to some caravan traders going down to Egypt (vv. 18, 28). In Egypt, Joseph was sold to Potiphar, the captain of Pharaoh's guard. He served Potiphar well and became steward of his household (39:1–4). But Potiphar's wife made illicit advances toward Joseph, which Joseph refused. Hell knows no fury like that of a woman scorned, so she accused him of attempted rape, and Joseph was thrown into prison (vv. 7–8, 14–15, 20).

While he was in prison, Joseph met Pharaoh's cupbearer and baker, who had displeased the king (40:1). During their time in prison, Joseph interpreted dreams for the cupbearer and baker, and both dreams came true (vv. 8–23). Sometime later, after the cupbearer had been restored, he told Pharaoh about Joseph's ability, and Pharaoh summoned Joseph to interpret his own dream (41:12–36). Pharaoh was so grateful, he appointed Joseph as the prime minister of Egypt, tasked with preparing for the famine Pharaoh had foreseen in his dream (vv. 37–45).

When the famine came upon the land, it affected Joseph's homeland, too. Jacob's family was starving, so Jacob sent some of his sons down to Egypt to buy some of the surplus food the prime minister had been wise enough to store away for the Egyptian people (42:1–2). When the sons went to Egypt, they encountered Joseph, but while they did not recognize him, he recognized them (vv. 6–8). Joseph hid his identity for a while, but finally revealed that he was their long-lost brother (45:3). At Joseph's invitation, Jacob moved his entire family to Egypt (46:5–7).

Years later, after Jacob had died, the brothers became afraid that Joseph would take revenge upon them for selling him into slavery (50:15). So, they concocted a story, saying that Jacob had told them that he wanted Joseph to forgive them (vv. 16–17). They need not have worried; Joseph had long since forgiven them. He said: "Do not fear, for am I in the place of God? As for you, you meant evil against me, but God meant it for good, to bring it about that many people should be kept alive, as they are today" (vv. 19–20).

Joseph did not whitewash the sin of his brothers. He said, "You meant evil against me." He was saying that they acted with evil intent in selling him to the Midianites. Like the Chaldeans, Joseph's brothers were guilty of sin, sin that they personally had wanted to do. But God stands above all human choices and works through human freedom to bring about His own providential goals. That is what Joseph was saying: "You chose to do something sinful, but all things work together for good to those who love God and are called according to His purpose. I'm called according to the purpose of God, and God has meant good through this." What good? First of all, God sent Joseph to Egypt to make preparations for the famine and thereby to save many lives, including those of his own family. Second, God caused Jacob's entire family to move to Egypt, that they might prosper there and multiply, only to be enslaved and later delivered by the mighty hand of God in one of the key moments of redemptive history. And God brought all this about through the concurrence of His own righteous will and the sinful will of Joseph's brothers.

GOD MEANT IT ALL FOR GOOD

There is an old, simple story that teaches a profound lesson: "For want of a nail, the shoe was lost. For want of the shoe, the horse was lost. For want of the horse, the rider was lost. For want of the rider, the message was lost. For want of the message, the battle was lost. For want of the battle, the kingdom was lost." What would have happened in the history of the world if Jacob had not given

Joseph a colorful coat? No coat, no jealousy. No jealousy, no treacherous sale of Joseph to Midianite traders. No sale of Joseph to Midianite traders, no descent into Egypt. No descent into Egypt, no meeting with Potiphar. No meeting with Potiphar, no trouble with his wife. No trouble with his wife, no imprisonment. No imprisonment, no interpretation of the dreams of Pharaoh. No interpretation of the dreams of Pharaoh, no elevation to the role of prime minister. No elevation to the role of prime minister, no reconciliation with his brothers. No reconciliation with his brothers, no migration of the Jewish people into Egypt. No migration into Egypt, no exodus out of Egypt. No exodus out of Egypt, no Moses, no law, no prophets—and no Christ! Do you think it was an accident in the plan of God that that coat happened? God meant it all for good.

Jonathan Edwards once preached a sermon entitled "God, the Author of All Good Volitions and Actions." I love that sermon title because it shows how unlike the average Christian Edwards was. Whenever we make good, noble, or virtuous choices, we like to assume all of the credit. On the other hand, if we do something that is not so good, something evil, we make excuses and pass off the blame. We do not want to take credit for our evil choices. We sometimes try to blame them on God, just as Adam did when he said, "The woman whom you gave to be with me, she gave me fruit of the tree, and I ate" (Gen. 3:12). He tried to blame the fall on God Himself. That's our tendency—take credit for the good, transfer blame for the evil. But Edwards understood that any good deed we do, any righteous choices that we make, are only because God is at work within us.

It is difficult to understand the relationship between God's providence and human freedom because man is truly free in the sense that he has the ability to make choices and to choose what he wants. But God is also truly free. This is why the Westminster Confession can say that God "freely" ordains everything without doing "violence . . . to the will of the creatures." Of course, if I've heard it once, I've heard it a thousand times: "God's sovereignty can never limit man's freedom." That is an expression of atheism, because if God's sovereignty is limited one ounce by our freedom, He is not sovereign. What kind of a concept of God do we have that we would say that God is paralyzed by human choices? If His freedom is limited by our freedom, we are sovereign, not God. No, we are free, but God is even more free. This means that our freedom can never limit God's sovereignty.

About the Author

Dr. R. C. Sproul is the founder and chairman of Ligonier Ministries, an international multimedia ministry based in Sanford, Florida. He also serves as senior minister of preaching and teaching at Saint Andrew's, a Reformed congregation in Sanford, and as president of Reformation Bible College, and his teaching can be heard around the world on the daily radio program *Renewing Your Mind.*

During his distinguished academic career, Dr. Sproul helped train men for the ministry as a professor at several theological seminaries.

He is the author of more than eighty books, including *The Holiness of God, Chosen by God, The Invisible Hand, Faith Alone, A Taste of Heaven, Truths We Confess, The Truth of the Cross,* and *The Prayer of the Lord.* He also served as general editor of *The Reformation Study Bible* and has written several children's books, including *The Prince's Poison Cup.*

Dr. Sproul and his wife, Vesta, make their home in Longwood, Florida.